Camino Packing List Guidebook

Camino Packing List Guidebook

For Your Pilgrimage to Santiago de Compostela

JEAN CHRISTIE ASHMORE

WALK FAR MEDIA
SEATTLE

© 2020 by Jean Christie Ashmore. All Rights Reserved

Contents

Part I. The Camino Backpack

1. Skin - Out   3
   What to Take on the Camino   3
2. Temptation   5
   Resist!   5
3. Backpack Size   7
   A Shopping Tip   7

Part II. Footwear

4. Hiking Footwear   13
   Boots vs. Sneakers vs. Trail Runners and More   13
5. Socks   17
   Thick or Thin   17
6. Alternate Footwear   19
   Cobblestones, Rest, Emergency   19

Part III. Clothing

7.	Walking Clothes	23
	Pleasant-Weather Hiking	23
8.	Extra Clothes	25
	Change is Good	25
9.	After the Camino Clothes	27
	Q: To Burn, or Not to Burn	27

Part IV. Weather Protection

10.	Rain Gear	31
	Options	31
11.	Staying Warm When It's Cold	33
	Creative Layering	33
12.	Staying Cool When It's Hot	35
	Protect Yourself	35

Part V. Sleeping Well

13.	Sleeping Bag	39
	Yes? No?	39
14.	Sleeping Sheet	41
	Yes? No?	41

15.	Creative Options	43
	Maybe?	43

Part VI. Small Items

16.	Toiletries	47
	Basics	47
17.	First Aid	51
	Essentials	51
18.	Blister Care	53
	Options	53

Part VII. Don't Forget These

19.	For Pockets	57
	Little Things That Matter	57
20.	Personal Stuff	59
	Ideas to Customize Your List	59
21.	Bags and Sacks	61
	How to Keep Your Backpack Contents Dry	61

Part VIII. Navigation

22.	Tech Devices	65
	Charging and Connectivity	65
23.	Camino Apps	69
	Yes! So Many...	69
24.	Guidebooks & Maps	71
	Print or Digital?	71

Part IX. The Complete 'Skin-Out' Camino Packing List

25.	A Packing Checklist for You	75

Part X. End Notes

26.	It Weighs How Much?!	91
27.	Customize Your Camino Backpack	94
28.	Contact, Copyright, Resources	97

PART I
THE CAMINO BACKPACK

1. Skin - Out

What to Take on the Camino

If you've not yet walked the Camino — this is for you.
It's a guidebook for what to take
on a Camino journey.

We'll start with the tips.

Then you'll get the packing list.
Absolutely everything is included.
In other words, it's a

'skin-out' packing list.

It's the same **checklist** that I use,
having fine-tuned it after walking
over 2,000 miles (3,200+ kilometers)
on Camino routes in France and Spain.

Happy Packing & Buen Camino!

Jean Christie
CaminoPackList.com/checklist

THE ESSENTIAL TIP

A lightweight Camino backpack weighs about 10-12% of your body weight when fully loaded.

Be sure to include water weight, and an estimated weight for picnic and snack foods for a realistic total backpack weight.

2. Temptation

Resist!

Most people want to get the 'big thing' first:
a Camino backpack.

But I encourage you to wait.
It's better to buy your Camino backpack

after

you've gathered all of your Camino gear.

Why?

Because then you'll know
the size, shape and features
to best fit the gear that you'll actually take.

~~~

CaminoPackList.com/checklist

3. Backpack Size

A Shopping Tip

To find the right backpack size:

1. Stuff all of your Camino gear into a large trash sack.

2. Take that sack with you to an outdoor gear store.

3. Shove the sack into different backpacks until it fits. (Allow a bit of extra room for picnic lunches, extra water, etc.)

Then, note the size of the pack if you want to shop online.

A Camino backpack's size typically falls in the **range of 35L to 50L** depending on your height and weight.

"L" means Liters.
It's the typical measurement for a **backpack's *interior volume capacity.***

~~~

You may also like

Camino De Santiago
To Walk Far, Carry Less

The classic book
used by thousands of Camino pilgrims
to learn how to create
the lightest possible Camino backpack.

**"Love this book!
My bible for the El Camino…"**
PINTEREST

~~~

WalkFarMedia.com *for more information.*

PART II
FOOTWEAR

4. Hiking Footwear

Boots vs. Sneakers vs. Trail Runners and More

A Frenchwoman insisted that her high-tech running shoes were the best shoes for the Camino.

A Spanish man pointed to his battered department-store sneakers and said, "These are the shoes you must wear for the Camino."

An American woman said wearing sports sandals with socks was the only way to walk the Camino.

A Basque man said his trail-hiking shoes were an excellent choice for the Camino journey.

A Frenchman who has walked thousands of kilometers on Camino routes—both popular and obscure—always wears his hiking boots.

~~~

Clearly, we can't say there's one type of footwear that's best for the Camino. Everyone has a different opinion.

But it's important to consider:

- **Rain** — get waterproof-breathable footwear (wet feet can cause blisters)
- **Comfort** — includes allowing extra room for your toes (try a half-size or a size larger than usual)
- **Durability** — get soles to last (Vibram® is a reputable brand name for quality soles)

Most of all, consider this: walking day-after-day for weeks. It's a different experience than weekend hikes.

Truly, the only way to know if your footwear will work well on the Camino is to start walking everyday to "audition" your footwear.

Walk on pavement (plenty of that on the Camino routes). Walk on dirt trails and rocky trails.

Walk uphill and downhill (going down steep hills is an excellent test to check the room for your toes). And walk in the rain — for hours if possible.

It's better to find footwear flaws at home — rather than on the Camino.

As previously discussed, don't get your Camino backpack first. Instead, get your hiking footwear first, then start walking — everyday if time allows.

Fifteen miles (about 24 Kms) is the average distance you'll walk each day on most Camino routes. So here's an important test: schedule at least one full day to walk at least fifteen miles (24 kilometers) on trails and/or on urban sidewalks.

it's better to find footwear flaws at home

You'll then have an excellent idea of what to expect on the Camino.

You'll also know how well your footwear (and walking clothes, rain gear, backpack, etc) might work for you.

~~~

CaminoPackList.com/checklist *for the best footwear*

———

> **THE ESSENTIAL TIP**
> Buy footwear before buying anything else.
> That way you can start training for the Camino — and test your footwear well in advance.

5. Socks

Thick or Thin

Just like footwear, there's no "best choice" when it comes to socks.

But whatever type of socks you choose, here are the most important features to look for:

- **No seams or flat seams** — avoid "bumpy" seams that rub your feet while you walk
- **Wicking properties** — to keep moisture away from your feet (moisture can cause blisters)
- **A good fit** — no excess material that will bunch in the toes or the heel

Also, shop for new footwear wearing the socks you expect to use. They'll affect how your footwear fits.

~~~

*See **CaminoPackList.com/checklist** for quality socks*

6. Alternate Footwear

Cobblestones, Rest, Emergency

Your alternate footwear has a few assignments. Wear them:

- **Inside pilgrim accommodations**
- **Outside during evening outings**
- **In communal showers**
- **As "emergency footwear"** (to continue hiking with painful blisters, for example)

Lightweight **sport sandals** are a common choice. They have stable soles (uneven cobblestones require some stability), can get wet, and can be worn with socks to keep your feet warm.

~~~

CaminoPacklist.com/checklist for alternate footwear ideas

PART III
CLOTHING

7. Walking Clothes

Pleasant-Weather Hiking

Hiking Pants: Most hikers wear "convertible" hiking pants (zip-off the legs to shorts or capris).

Shirt: Long sleeves offer just enough warmth (e.g against early-morning coolness) and will also protect your arms from insect bites and sunburn.

Underwear: I recommend 3 pair so you can take a night (or two) off from doing hand-wash laundry.

Socks: Also 3 pair — same reason as the "undies."

Hat: I recommend "bucket" style hats. They're lightweight and "crushable" (to easily fit inside a pocket). Get a wide-enough brim to cover your ears and shade your nose.

~~~

CaminoPackList.com/checklist for recommended bucket hats and hiking clothes.

8. Extra Clothes

Change is Good

- **Extra long-sleeve shirt**
  T-shirt — or a shirt with a collar. Collar advantage: it protects your neck from sunburn; or keeps the neck warm when it's windy-cold
- **A short-sleeve T-shirt**
  To sleep in, or to wear while hiking (beware the sun on your arms for hours...)
- **Three pairs of socks: another advantage**
  Put on a clean pair of socks at midday, when feet are sweaty (to help prevent blisters)
- **Three pair of underwear: another advantage**
  Ladies, this could happen to you too: squatting in the weeds without noticing the burrs below...
- **An extra pair of pants; or...**
  Capris or a skirt or a kilt

~~~

9. After the Camino Clothes

Q: To Burn, or Not to Burn

Some pilgrims continue to walk onward from Santiago de Compostela to Finisterre on the Atlantic coast ("the end of the earth").

And some go for this ritual:

to burn their well-worn Camino clothes on the shores of the Atlantic Ocean.

This marks the end of a journey, and the start of something new.

I don't recommend carrying clean clothing for the entire distance of your Camino journey.

Santiago de Compostela has many shops to buy new clothing to wear after "the burn."

~~~

CaminoApps.com *for Finisterre route apps*

> **Tip for Women**
> Sometimes men's outdoor gear have better features
> (deeper pockets, sturdier zippers)
> and also have a "baggier" fit that works well for layering.

PART IV
WEATHER PROTECTION

10. Rain Gear

Options

Plan on rain, no matter the route you take — or the time of year you walk. Whether it's blisters caused by wet feet or the danger of hypothermia — the consequences of being out in the open for hours without rain protection can be awful.

The basics: poncho or rain jacket; rain pants; and a rain cover for your backpack.

Some people use gaiters (not rain pants) to keep their socks dry when wearing shorts under a poncho in the warm summer rains.

I discuss, in depth, the pros and cons of a poncho vs. a rain jacket in the book *To Walk Far, Carry Less.*

~~~

CaminoPackList.com/checklist for recommended rain gear

11. Staying Warm When It's Cold

Creative Layering

Once, during an unexpected spring snowstorm, I wore a fleece ear band over a lightweight bucket hat under a jacket hood. Really, really cute.

The point: ditch vanity. Wear what you've got to stay warm. In the spring or fall, consider taking...

- **A down vest, a puff-jacket, *or* a fleece jacket**
- **Waterproof baseball-style hat** — the hat's brim helps keep a jacket or poncho's hood from collapsing around your face (better vision in windy-rainy weather)
- **Long underwear bottoms** – sleep in them, or wear under hiking pants or rain pants
- **Little things matter:** rainproof gloves, fleece ear band, fleece sherpa-style hat, baggy socks to keep feet warm at night

~~~

12. Staying Cool When It's Hot

Protect Yourself

- **Long-sleeve baggy shirts** (men & women)
- **Capris or shorts — skirts or kilts**
  Be mindful of avoiding sunburned legs
- **Water, Water, Water**
  It weighs a lot, but it's so essential to your well-being. The water-weight diminishes as the day progresses. Start out with a lot (2 Liters minimum)
- **Hat:** you'll need enough of a brim to shade your ears, face and neck
- **Tip:** keep a clean bandana in your pocket, pour water on it, and wipe your face and neck for instant coolness (one day it was so hot I did this every 10-15 minutes while walking)

~~~

> **The Essential Tip**
> Wise pilgrims plan for rain — even in the summer.

PART V
SLEEPING WELL

13. Sleeping Bag

Yes? No?

This is a topic of much discussion and debate among those walking the Camino.
(I discuss, in depth, the pros and cons of a sleeping bag vs. sleeping sheet in the book To Walk Far, Carry Less).

Here's my choice: I *always* take a lightweight sleeping bag (*less* than 2 lbs (about .90 kg)

Here's why: I like having a cozy sleeping bag with me. After a long day's hike, it's nice to know that, no matter what the accommodation situation is, I'll at least have my own bedding with me. If there's an overflow crowd at an albergue that's sleeping on a local school's gym floor, I'd rather have a sleeping bag than not.

If there's an overflow crowd...

There's this too: although camping is not allowed on Camino routes, there are times I've 'fallen asleep" for the night somewhere along the trail. For example, a few pilgrims and I once "fell asleep" under a 2000 year old Roman arch. Another night, a friend and I fell asleep under the stars, while lying with our backs against the sun-warmed stones of an old country chapel.

I once fell asleep under a 2000 year old Roman arch

Lately, I also bring a lightweight foam pad. Before leaving home, I cut it to fit the size between my shoulders and knees. That reduces the weight even more. A foam pad is perfect for picnics, siestas, and when sleeping in "overflow" accommodations like a gym floor.

~~~

CaminoPackList.com/checklist *for Sleeping Gear options*
Get the book **To Walk Far, Carry Less** *to learn more*

14. Sleeping Sheet

Yes? No?

It depends mostly on luck...

I once walked a 500 mile route in France with just a traveler's silk sleeping-sheet.

I loved not having the bulk of a sleeping bag in my backpack. And, my backpack was about 1.5 pounds (about .68 kg) lighter-in-weight too (about the weight of my sleeping bag). Sweet!

But sometimes there were no blankets left in the group accommodations to cover my thin sleeping sheet. That can happen a lot in Spain too.

See **The Bottom Line** on the next page...

~~~

CaminoPackList.com for sleeping gear options
Get the book To Walk Far, Carry Less *to learn more*

The Essential Tip
Avoid using "loud"
rustling, crunching, crackling
plastic bags to organize your gear.
Then you won't disturb your fellow
sleeping pilgrims
in group accommodations.

15. Creative Options

Maybe?

- **a lightweight down-throw** (to use with a sleeping sheet, or a travel sheet)
- **a sleeping bag liner** (some are heavier than others, worth considering for the hot summer months)

The Bottom Line

When it comes to the choices between a sleeping bag, sleeping sheet, or other options — it's really this:

Will you feel ok taking the chance that you'll always find a blanket when you need one?

~~~

CaminoPackList.com/checklist *for sleeping gear options*
Get the book **To Walk Far, Carry Less** *to learn more*

PART VI
SMALL ITEMS

16. Toiletries

Basics

Get travel sizes, because ounces and grams quickly add up to pounds and kilograms. It's easy to replenish supplies along the way.

And: a zip-lock baggie is lighter-in-weight than a fabric toiletry bag.

Naturally, you'll want to choose your own toiletries.

But here are the basics, with some notes:

- **Toothbrush – Toothpaste – Dental Floss**
- **Deodorant**
- **Comb or Brush**
- **Soap bar for hair, body, and clothes** – Mild, natural ingredient soap bars work great for everything.
- **Microfiber pack towel** – A lightweight backpacker or traveler's towel
- **Microfiber face cloth** -Not essential, but nice. I got mine with the soap bar mentioned above. About 4" x 5" square. Lighter-in-weight

than an ordinary wash-cloth.
- **Toilet paper** – travel-size roll — 55 sheets
- **Pads or tampons** – Only a few — can easily buy more along the way
- **Toenail clippers** – Long-distance walkers can avoid problems by keeping toenails clipped short

> **You can count on loud snoring. Not by you of course.**

- **2 clothespins** – Most of the pilgrim accommodations will have some; but it's handy to have your own to hang underwear and socks each night. Pants and shirts can fold over the clotheslines.
- **Earplugs!** – I always add the exclamation mark because this is an essential item: you can count on loud snoring in pilgrim accommodations along Camino routes.
Not by you, of course.

~~~

CaminoPackList.com/checklist for links to handmade soap bars for hair, body and light laundry

*

SWISS MINIMALISM

The most creative
lightweight backpacking gear ever:
pantyhose!

A Swiss woman
brought them with her
for unexpected cold temperatures.

17. First Aid

Essentials

Backpacker's First Aid kit: Prepare your own, or buy one. I recommend the latter, because they're so compact and comprehensive.

Scissors (small): Useful for a variety of situations, including cutting bandage rolls. But, like the pocket knife in your food bag, you may need to buy this abroad (airport security limits).

My small *folding* scissors have, so far, made it through security.

Pain Relievers: Take small quantities. You can easily buy these in France and Spain at pharmacies along the way.

Hand Sanitizer: Can also replenish along the way. Useful before picnic lunches and for general use during the day.

~~~

CaminoPackList.com/checklist for a link to small folding scissors, and a small backpacker's first aid kit

18. Blister Care

Options

Blister treatment and prevention options: what works for some people, will not work for others. Duct tape? Not for me!

These are my favorites:

- **Gentle paper tape** – Put the tape on when you first feel a "hot spot" developing — *before* you get a blister.
- **Compeed** – although this brand of blister bandages has its drawbacks, they're useful for early to moderate stage blisters.
- **Toe gel caps** – excellent to help prevent or cover blisters.

Start the Camino with your favorite blister care items. You might need them on day one…

~~~

CaminoPackList.com/checklist *for links to blister prevention and treatment choices*

PART VII
DON'T FORGET THESE

19. For Pockets

Little Things That Matter

Several "little things" are not listed here, but are included in the packing-list checklist. They're obvious items that don't need any comments or explanations.

Mobile phone – nearly everyone has one, but they're not essential, only useful

Whistle – to confuse aggressive dogs

A small memo pad & pen – a local person can quickly draw a map to the trail, or to a bar/cafe, or to a hotel. Or, you can leave a note on the trail for someone if you can't text them; or you can warn anonymous fellow pilgrims behind you: "Bridge washed out up ahead. Turn left here instead."

Bandana: – this is such a versatile, useful item, you'll be happy to have a couple of them with you. A caution: the cheapest bandanas may bleed their colors. My white shirt turned green around the collar. Ruined!

Wallet for Euro bills and a Coin purse – Euro coins are large, and they're used a lot — so a separate container is useful. A wallet helps you to avoid using your money belt in public.

Money belt (don't ever leave unattended in your backpack)

Recommended for safekeeping of your passport, credit cards, and large bills. It's uncomfortable to wear it while hiking, but don't leave it in your backpack unattended—even for a moment. I've heard about thieves snatching backpacks. It happens fast.

Tuck the money belt somewhere safe while sleeping in group accommodations, like inside the foot of your sleeping bag. While showering, keep it with you in a plastic bag.

For specific information on Camino Safety, visit WalkFarMedia.com

~~~

CaminoPackList.com/checklist for useful small things, including a "pocket pack" and quality bandanas that won't bleed their colors

20. Personal Stuff

Ideas to Customize Your List

- **Pilgrim's credential** –*A MUST-HAVE-ITEM* *if you want to sleep in Camino pilgrim accommodations. Get them at popular Camino starting points — or contact your country's Camino pilgrim association*
- **Scallop Shell** – a Camino tradition: hanging a scallop shell from your backpack. You can easily get them along the Camino (or you can get a shell patch to sew onto your backpack instead)
- **Personal essentials:** prescription medicine, a knee brace, extra eyeglasses, a copy of your prescriptions, travel insurance documents
- **Artists** bring items particular to their work – sketch pads, cameras, watercolors
- **Lightweight print or ebooks:** I highly recommend *The Art of Pilgrimage: The Seeker's Guide to Making Travel Sacred by Phil Cousineau*

~~~

THE ESSENTIAL TIP

Zip-lock bags (gallon-size)
are excellent for organizing things
inside your backpack.

They make it easy
to find things at a glance.

21. Bags and Sacks

How to Keep Your Backpack Contents Dry

To *always* keep your backpack and it's contents dry:

- Line the *inside* of your pack with a large trash sack
- Use a Backpack rain-cover on the *outside* of your backpack

Organizational bags and sacks: It's easy to find stuff in your backpack using **clear plastic bags, colored bags, or mesh bags.**

Also useful**:** a **pocket-pack** (mini-backpack), or a **drawstring bag** – take valuables, bottle of water, etc. with you while sightseeing or eating out at night. Also useful for carrying food after shopping.

~~~

CaminoPackList.com/checklist for backpack rain covers, pocket-packs, and stuff sacks

PART VIII
NAVIGATION

22. Tech Devices

Charging and Connectivity

I first walked the Camino in 2001. I carried no technology — not even a camera. Nothing to charge, nothing to keep track of, and no serious worries about my backpack ever getting lost or stolen.

I was outside of time, in a far-away place. It was a liberty. There was a sense of stillness, even while walking. The Camino is an excellent opportunity to unplug, shut-down, and disconnect for a deeply quiet, alone-in-the-world, experience.

Alas — I'm also in love with the technology of today. My iPhone has dramatically increased my options (to find places to stay, transportation options, lightweight digital guidebooks and maps, GPS, compass, messaging, etc.). And it's a fine camera too.

> **I was outside of time, in a far-away place.**

I mention all of this to remind you that, not too long

ago, everyone wandered the Camino without tech devices. And things worked out just fine...

Back to reality...most people want to bring their mobile phones. Yes, you'll usually have cellular coverage everywhere. Yes, you can charge your devices in pilgrim accommodations. Yes, WiFi is fairly easy to find. Yes, there are specific Camino route apps (go to **CaminoApps.com**).

I recommend taking these things:

- **a portable power charger** (in group accommodations it's safer to leave that alone to charge, rather than your mobile phone)
- **a plug adapter** (if needed: Spain and France may have different power outlets than your country)
- **getting a pay-as-you-go SIM card** (purchased locally in Spain, France, or Portugal – it makes phone calls local, therefore less expensive. Data use is typically cheaper too.)

~~~

CaminoPackList.com/checklist for recommended portable chargers and plug adapters

THE ESSENTIAL TIP

Ask your phone carrier for reduced pricing
for international data and calling plans
unless your mobile phone is "unlocked."

If it is unlocked,
you can buy local SIM cards
for less expensive calling and data rates.

Either way,
you'll have more money
to eat tapas.

23. Camino Apps

Yes! So Many...

You'll find countless app choices for both Android and iPhone mobile phones, *including*:

- **route apps** for nearly all of the organized Spanish Camino routes (including the Camino Portugués and its route variants)
- **transportation apps** for Spanish, French and other European rail, bus, airline, ride-share, and taxi options
- **accommodation apps** for everywhere in Europe
- **guidebook apps** for Spain, France, Portugal (among other countries)
- **language and translation** apps, and dictionary apps too

There are also apps for specific locations or places, such as the **audio guide for the Cathedral of Santiago de Compostela;** and an app to explore **the beaches of Northern Spain,** if you're planning on walking the Camino del Norte.

You can even get the official **Spanish government's weather-app**, to see the most localized source of weather information.

And, among the specialty apps, you'll find **apps to help vegetarians and vegans** discover restaurants and cafes across Europe.

~~~

*Go to **CaminoApps.com** for curated lists of Camino apps.*

24. Guidebooks & Maps

Print or Digital?

Advantage Digital: *Apps and/or ebooks* don't add weight to your backpack.

Disadvantage Digital: *Apps and/or ebooks* can only be accessed on a mobile phone that is charged — and, in some cases, must have connectivity to either wireless or cellular networks.

Advantage Print: *paperback guidebooks and paper maps* never need charging…

Disadvantage Print: *paperback guidebooks and paper maps* add weight to your backpack.

Tip: *A general-orientation map of western Europe is useful for planning too.*

~~~

CaminoApps.com — CaminoPackList.com

PART IX
THE COMPLETE 'SKIN-OUT' CAMINO PACKING LIST

25. A Packing Checklist for You

Clothing

[ ] Pants x 2 pair (optional: one pair are capris)

[ ] Shirt with pockets (long-sleeve)

[ ] T-Shirt or another shirt (long-sleeve)

[ ] T-shirt (short-sleeve)

[ ] Sports bra

[ ] Underpants x 3 pair

[ ] Socks x 3 pair

[ ] Layer for warmth (light-fleece or down)

[ ] Hiking footwear

CaminoPackList.com/checklist — the best Camino gear

Rain Gear

[ ] Rain hat

[ ] Waterproof jacket *or* a poncho

[ ] Rain Pants

[ ] Gaiters (optional)

For the pros & cons of rain gear choices read Camino de Santiago: To Walk Far, Carry Less

Other Clothing

[ ] Alternate footwear

[ ] Sun hat

If cooler weather expected:

[ ] Waterproof gloves

[ ] Ear band, beanie, or sherpa-style hat

[ ] Long underwear (bottoms) or leggings
— *some use for sleeping, along with the short-sleeve T-shirt listed above*

[ ] Baggy pair of socks for cold feet while sleeping

CaminoPacklist.com/checklist

Sleeping Gear

[ ] Sleeping bag, sheet or other option

[ ] Foam pad (or other *lightweight* pad – Optional)

*For the pros & cons of sleeping gear options
read Camino de Santiago: To Walk Far, Carry Less*

~~~

Toiletries

[ ] Toothbrush

[ ] Toothpaste

[ ] Dental floss

[ ] Deodorant

[ ] Soap bar (multi-purpose)

[ ] Comb and/or brush

[ ] Microfiber pack towel

[ ] Microfiber face cloth

[ ] Travel-size toilet paper roll

[ ] Toe-nail clippers

[ ] Clothespins x 2

[ ] Earplugs

[ ] A *tiny* flashlight for nighttime bathroom visits

CaminoPackList.com/checklist — *the best Camino gear*

~~~

First Aid

[ ] Backpacker's first-aid kit

[ ] Small, folding scissors

[ ] Hand-sanitizer spray

[ ] Pain-reliever

Other:

[ ] Prescription drugs and copy of prescriptions

[ ] Knee brace (optional)

Blister Care

[ ] Your preferred blister-care items
— enough to cover the first few walking days — you can replenish these at pharmacies along the way

CaminoPackList.com/checklist — the best backpacker first aid kit

~~~

Little Things for Pants or Backpack Pockets

[ ] Bandanas x 2 (one for your food sack; one for a backpack pocket)

[ ] Lip balm

[ ] Sunscreen

[ ] Tissues

[ ] Gum/Mints

[ ] Wallet for Euros (daily spending)

[ ] Coin purse for Euro coins

[ ] Whistle (to confuse aggressive dogs)

[ ] Memo pad & pen

[ ] Sunglasses; Reading glasses

[ ] Pocket language dictionary (optional — useful when offline)

CaminoPackList.com/checklist — the best Camino gear

~~~

Tech Gear

Possibilities:

[ ] Mobile phone

[ ] Charging cord

[ ] Adapter plug(s)

[ ] Portable charger

[ ] Earbuds

[ ] Wristwatch

Guidebook & Maps

[ ] Camino route guidebook

[ ] Camino route map

[ ] General orientation map of Western Europe (optional)

CaminoPackList.com/checklist — the best portable chargers and adapter plugs

~~~

Personal Stuff

[ ] Pilgrim's credential

[ ] Money Belt

[ ] Passport, Credit Cards

[ ] Trekking Poles

[ ] Scallop shell

[ ] Small & lightweight notebook for journal

[ ] Small spoon

[ ] Pocket knife

[ ] Extra pair of prescription eyeglasses or copy of your prescription

[ ] Tampons or pads (can easily replenish along the way)

[ ] Artist tools and supplies

[ ] Meaningful to You: an important book; something (a small stone?) to mark a moment or to memorialize someone along the Camino

~~~

Bags & Sacks

[ ] Pocket-pack (mini-backpack) or a drawstring bag

[ ] Large trash sack (for interior of backpack)

[ ] Food bag

[ ] Alternate-shoes bag

[ ] Zip-lock bags as needed

[ ] Mesh bag or colored bags for clothing

Backpack

[ ] Backpack with features to fit your stuff and suit your needs

[ ] Backpack rain cover

[ ] Hydration system; or water bottles

For pros & cons of hydration systems vs water bottles get the book Camino de Santiago: To Walk Far, Carry Less

~~~

OTHER ITEMS (You Want To Take)

[ ]

_____

[ ]

_____

[ ]

_____

[ ]

_____

[ ]

_____

[ ]

_____

~~~

OTHER ITEMS (You Want To Take)

[ ]

[ ]

[ ]

[ ]

[ ]

[ ]

~~~

NOTES

~~~

NOTES

~~~

PART X
END NOTES

26. It Weighs How Much?!

Food and Water

It's important to consider how much food and water will weigh in a Camino backpack. That way, when you weigh your fully-loaded backpack, you'll be able to add an estimate for a *realistic* backpack total weight.

Water is always the single biggest weight hog in your backpack. But even a few snack or picnic foods add a surprising amount of weight too.

Water is always the biggest weight hog

To illustrate this point, here's the amount of water I usually start out with, and also what I typically carry in my food bag:

- **2 liters of water** (depending on water access during each day's walk, 1 liter of water may suffice)
  4 ½ pounds (about 2 kilograms)
- **1 banana, apple, or an orange** (average weight

for one piece of fruit) **7 ounces (200 grams).**
- **Bread and cheese** (a light lunch)
  just over 1 pound (454 grams)
- **Bag of almonds** (snack)
  4.6 ounces (130 grams)Add some basic utensils:
- **Small spoon**
  0.06 ounce (17 grams)
- **Small Pocketknife**
  1.3 ounces (36 grams)

Add some "emergency" food items (for when shops and restaurants are closed — or if there are none):

- **1 energy bar**
  1.8 ounces (53 grams)
- **2 tea bags**
  0.02 ounce (6 grams)
- **1 packet of instant soup**
  0.7 ounce (20 grams)

Carry food in a leak-proof bag:

- **Ziplock plastic bag**
  (to hold emergency food items)
- **Food bag** (to hold all food and utensils)
  2 ounces (59 grams) for both bags

Total Estimated Food & Water weight:
6.6 pounds (2.99 kilograms)

You can see that even a basic amount of food and water adds a lot to the total weight of your backpack.

The good news: as the day continues you'll consume most of the water and food. So, at the end of the day when you're most fatigued, your backpack will weigh a lot less.

~~~

More in-depth advice to lighten your load: To Walk Far, Carry Less

27. Customize Your Camino Backpack

To Walk Far, Carry Less

If you've never backpacked before, it's essential to learn how experienced backpackers create a *lightweight* backpack.

I've seen countless Camino pilgrims stop their journey to Santiago because of issues related to a far-too heavy backpack — like Achilles tendonitis, chronic knee issues, or persistent (and sometimes bleeding and infected) blisters.

It's been my goal to share with others what I learned after backpacking over 2,000 miles. My hope is that you'll feel increasingly fit day-after-day — instead of feeling worn-out and discouraged to the point of giving up.

Readers have told me that what they liked most of all is how *To Walk Far Carry Less* helped them make *informed choices* when preparing their Camino backpack.

Rain jacket or poncho? Water bottles or a pack hydration system? Sleeping bag or sleeping sheet? I cover the pros and cons for the most debatable gear. And offer advice to help you consider your options. Then you'll be able to decide what works best for you.

Thousands of Camino pilgrims have used To Walk Far, Carry Less to create their own customized — and lightweight — Camino backpack.

 WalkFarMedia.com for links to the book in print, Kindle, or ebook formats.

28. Contact, Copyright, Resources

Camino Packing List Guidebook
For Your Pilgrimage to Santiago de Compostela

Copyright © 2020 by Jean Christie Ashmore
All Rights Reserved.

ISBN 978-0-9837580-3-7   print book
ISBN 978-0-9837580-4-4 ebook

Published in the United States of America

For permissions please contact:
www.WalkFarMedia.com

Walk Far Media
— Seattle —

Websites

CaminoApps.com
The best apps for the Camino
CaminoPackList.com
The best hiking gear for the Camino
WalkFarMedia.com
Get Fit for Life. Again.
WalkFarMedia.thinkific.com
Online Courses for Fun & Good Health

Books

Camino de Santiago: To Walk Far, Carry Less
The classic book used by thousands to create a lightweight Camino backpack.

Easy Bread Making:
A Simple Recipe to Bake Your Own Bread
Bonus: learn how to make your own specialty breads.
Example: apricot-walnut bread.
Ages 10 yrs.+

Online Courses

The Quit Smoking Game™
For you. For someone you love.
It works.

———

Easy Bread Making
An Online Course

———

How to Do a Card Trick
They'll Never, Ever Guess How to Do
For Grandparents, Aunts, Uncles and Parents
Friends & Colleagues
And kids ages 9+

——————

Register at
WalkFarMedia.thinkific.com

Thank you for purchasing

Camino Packing List Guidebook
For Your Pilgrimage to Santiago de Compostela

**It's an enormous help to authors
when you review our books.**

I'd be grateful if you'd take the time now
to let me and future readers know
if you liked this book.

**It really does help us all
when you review books!**

Thank you, and Buen Camino!
♡

Jean Christie

Made in United States
North Haven, CT
06 March 2023

33693012R00065